Music Minus One Piano

Edward MacDowell

Concerto No. 2 for Piano and Orchestra in D minor, Op. 23

SUGGESTIONS FOR USING THIS MMO EDITION

WE HAVE TRIED to create a product that will provide you an easy way to learn and perform this concerto with a full orchestra in the comfort of your own home. Because it involves a fixed orchestral performance, there is an inherent lack of flexibility in tempo and cadenza length. The following MMO features and techniques will reduce these inflexibilities and help you maximize the effectiveness of the MMO practice and performance system:

Where the soloist begins a movement *solo*, we have provided an introductory measure with subtle taps inserted at the actual tempo before the soloist's entrance. Taps have also been inserted in two places in the accompaniment version as tempo guides during difficult tempo changes.

Chapter stops on your CD are conveniently located throughout the piece at the beginnings of practice sections, and are cross-referenced in the score. This should help you quickly find a desired place in the music as you learn the piece.

Chapter stops have also been placed at orchestra entrances (after cadenzas, for example) so that, with the help of a second person, it is possible to perform a seamless version of the concerto alongside your MMO CD accompaniment. While we have allotted what is generally considered an average amount of time for a cadenza, each performer will have a different interpretation and observe individual tempi. Your personal rendition may preclude a perfect "fit" within the space provided. Therefore, by having a second person press the pause‖button on your CD player after the start of each cadenza, followed by the next track▸▸button, your CD will be cued to the orchestra's re-entry. When you as soloist are at the end of the cadenza or other solo passage, the second person can press the play▸(or pause‖button) on the CD remote to allow a synchronized orchestra re-entry.

Regarding tempi: we have observed generally accepted tempi, but some may wish to perform at a different tempo, or to slow down or speed up the accompaniment for practice purposes. You can purchase from MMO (or from other audio and electronics dealers) specialized CD players which allow variable speed while maintaining proper pitch. This is an indispensable tool for the serious musician and you may wish to look into purchasing this useful piece of equipment for full enjoyment of all your MMO editions.

We want to provide you with the most useful practice and performance accompaniments possible. If you have any suggestions for improving the MMO system, please feel free to contact us. You can reach us by e-mail at info@musicminusone.com.

EDWARD MACDOWELL

CONCERTO № 2

IN D MINOR

FOR

PIANO & ORCHESTRA

OP. 23

Edward MacDowell's Piano Concerto No. 2 in D minor, op. 23

Edward MacDowell was born in 1860, twelve years after the Norwegian composer Edvard Grieg. He was a contemporary of Russian composer Anton Arensky, and French master Claude Debussy. Grieg, Arensky, Debussy and MacDowell all owe something to Liszt and Chopin, and represent late Romantic Nationalism at its best.

In the Arensky Concerto, which I recorded earlier for Music Minus One, it is easy to hear the derivations of his material: the Chopin Concerto No. 2 in the same key of F minor, the Grieg Concerto (the theme of the Arensky's last movement steals Grieg's famous motto), and the Liszt E-flat Concerto No. 1, with trills and triangle. The MacDowell, however, is far more subtle, having a spiritual kinship without actually copying material from other works. Indeed, MacDowell's originality of conception and peculiarly American style makes this work, in my view, a true masterpiece of its kind. The technical and musical challenges are considerable. It was written for Theresa Carreño, the Martha Argerich of her day, and thus the expectations were for a virtuoso command. It is possible to take slower than required tempi and ease the burdens somewhat, but the work really requires whirlwind speed for the second and third movements. Among the challenges are powerful and fast octaves, extended passagework, double notes, trills and excellent tonal control at all dynamic ranges. I find it more challenging than the Grieg or Arensky concerti and equal to the two Liszt.

The first movement requires a firm grasp of the form in order to keep it from disintegrating into sections. Pay attention to the tempo fluctuations and don't let them become too great. *Poco più* or *meno mosso*. I omitted many of the pedal markings from Edwin Hughes' 1922 edition (though some may want to consult them for further study). Use your own creativity and judgment, but keep a rich and warm sonority in mind always.

I have given individual performance suggestions and notes throughout the score as footnotes for easy reference.

—*Paul Van Ness*

SECOND CONCERTO
for Piano and Orchestra
in D minor, op. 23

Edited by Paul Van Ness

Edward MacDowell
(1860-1908)

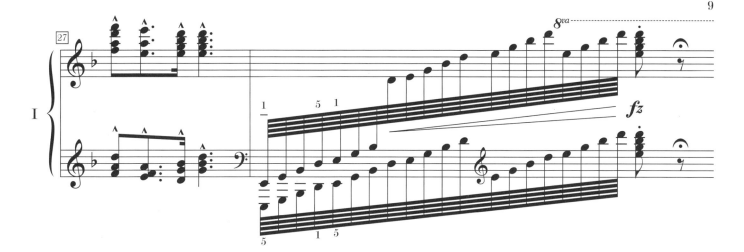

Poco più mosso, e con passione ♩. = *60* *)

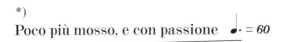

Poco più mosso, e con passione ♩. = *60*

*) At bar 49, the accompaniment must be soft but distinct; the clarity adds sweep to the melodic contour.

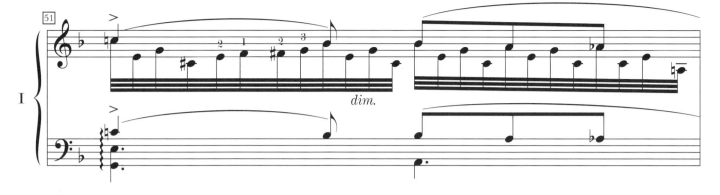

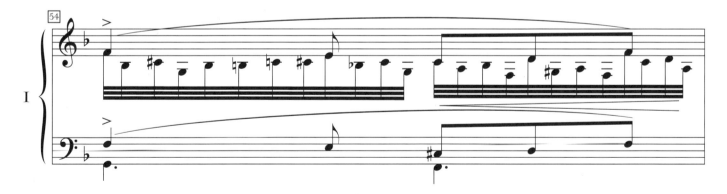

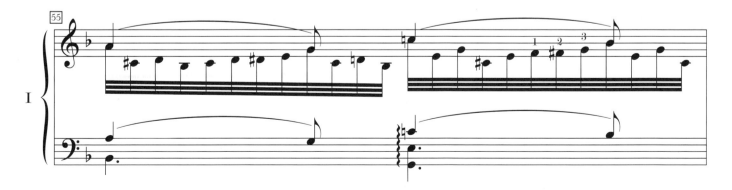

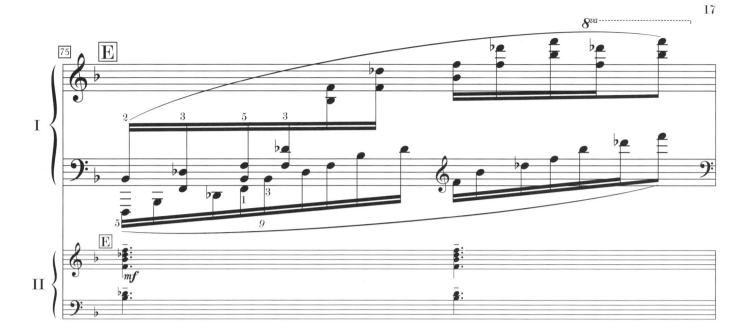

*) This difficult passage at bar 77 requires exploration of various fingerings if you are to maintain tempo and get all the notes. Some people actually play the first half measure as duplet 32nds. It doesn't sound too bad and is better than dragging the tempo in order to get "all the notes."

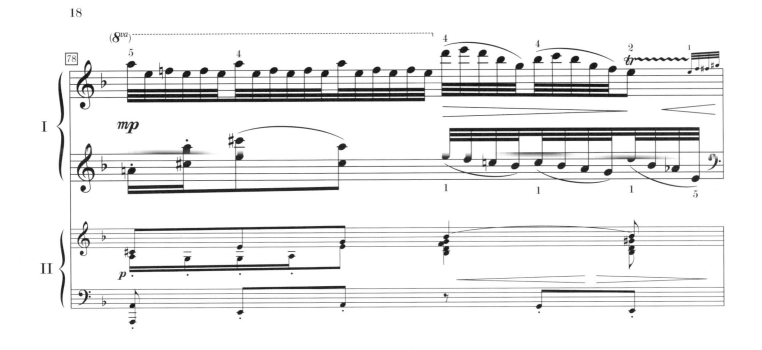

*) At bar 83, Tempo I is the *Larghetto*, not the *poco più mosso*.

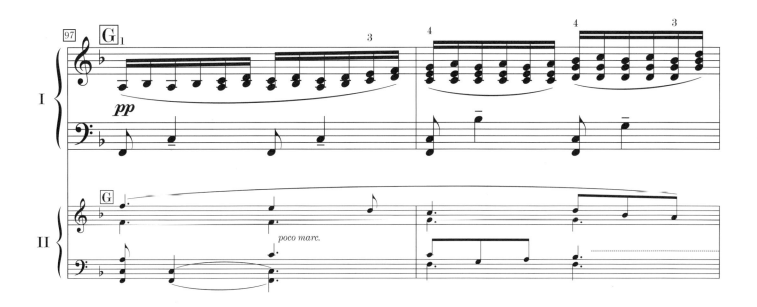

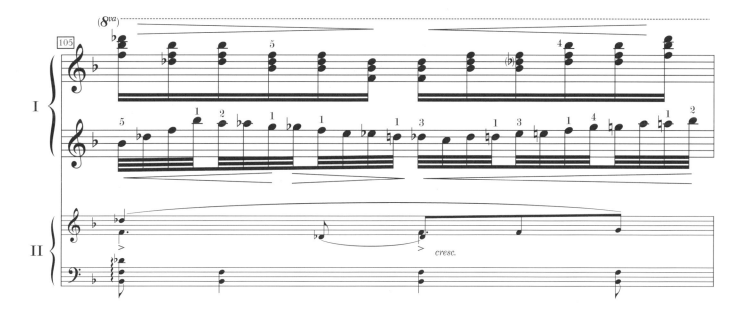

*) At bar 109, the conductor should give you a little time to get there!

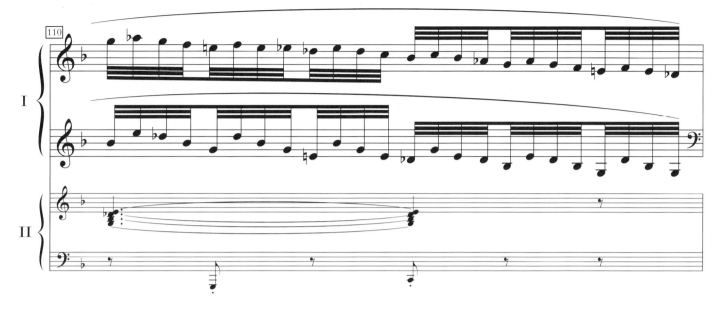

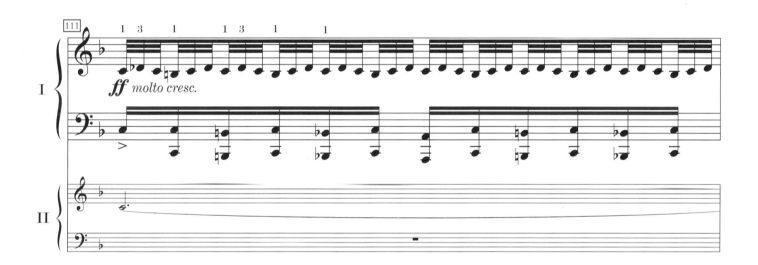

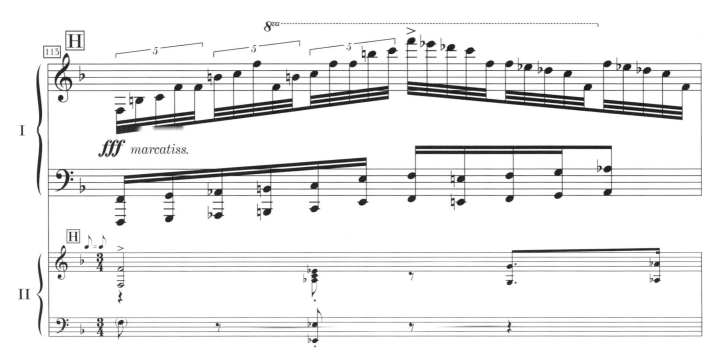

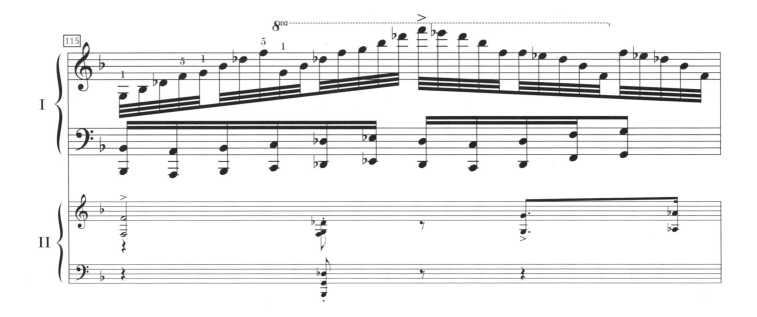

*)

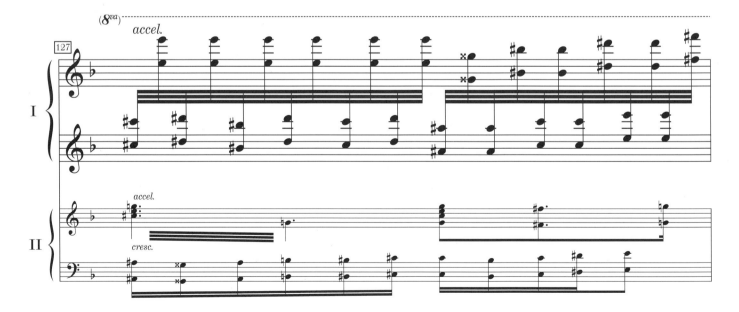

*) At bar 125 I like to push the tempo earlier than the marked accelerando. At bar 127, the conductor should follow.

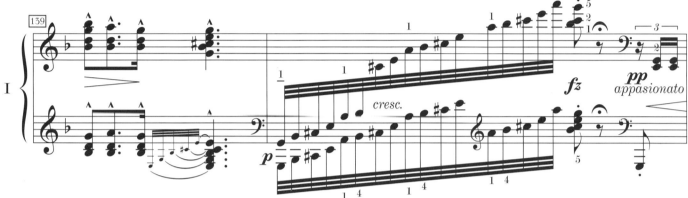

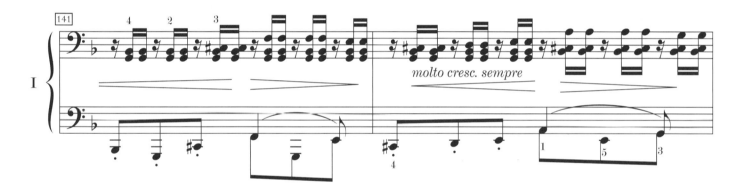

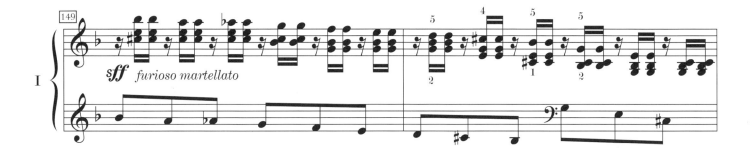

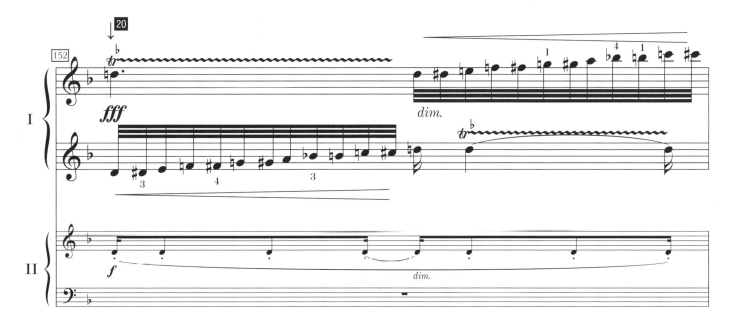

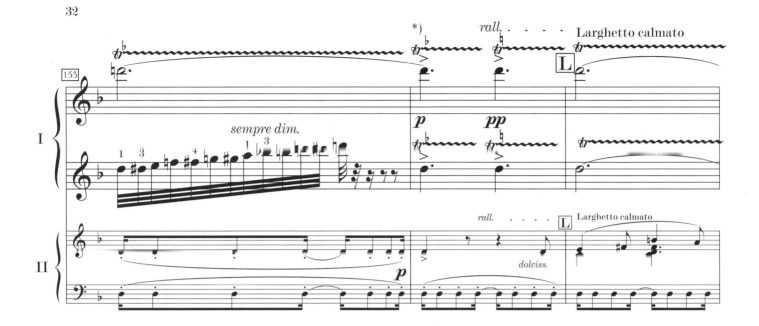

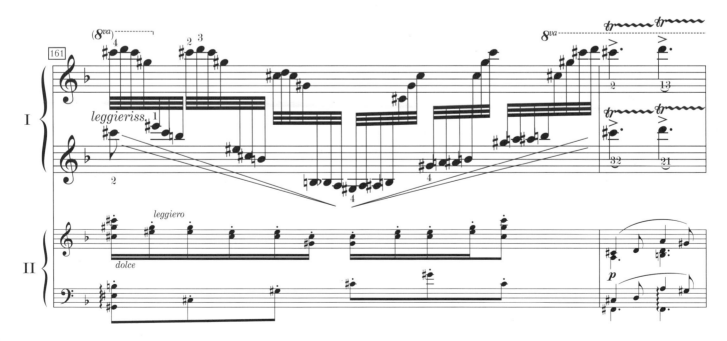

*) At bar 154 stay in tempo until the middle of the bar and let the orchestra make the rallentando.

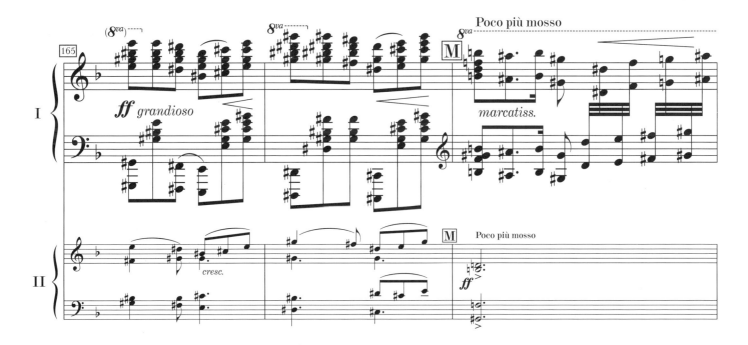

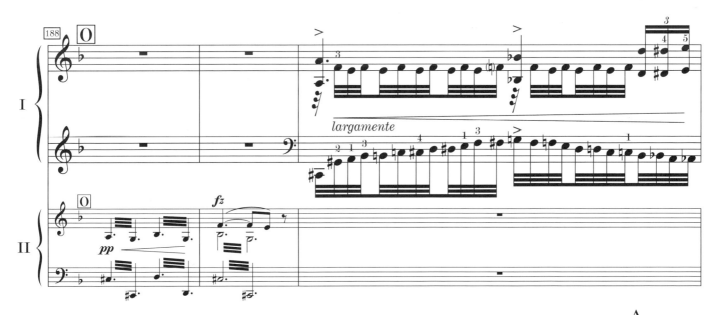

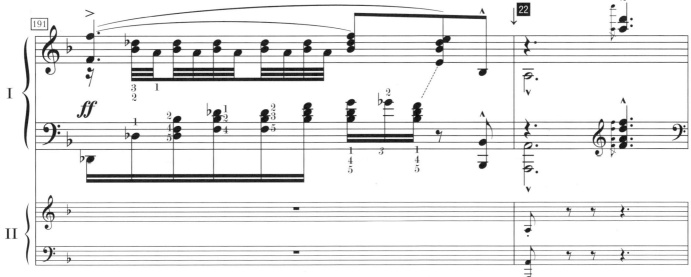

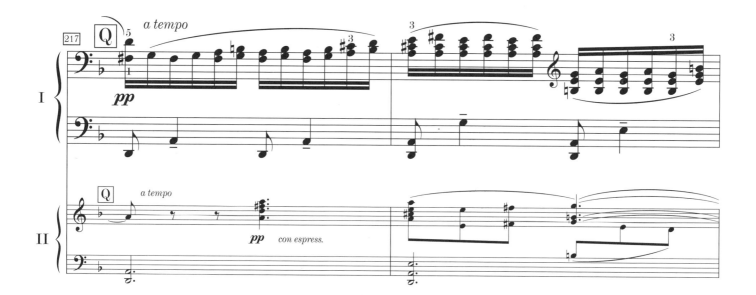

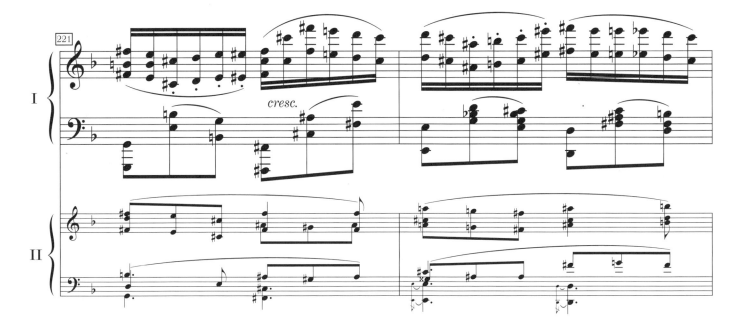

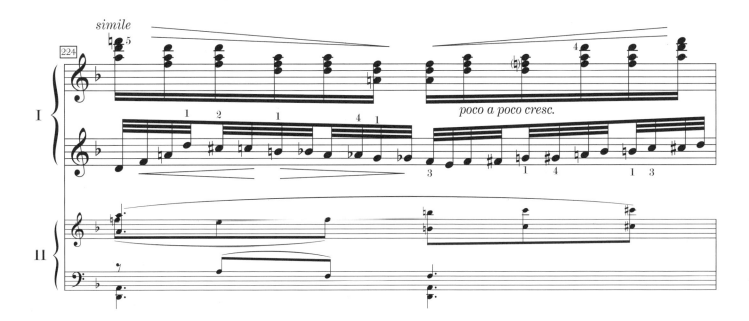

40

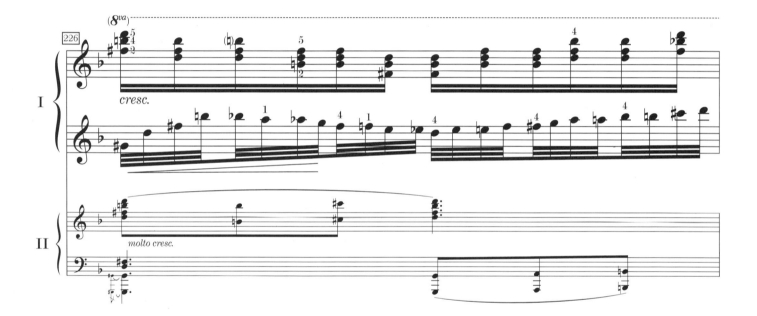

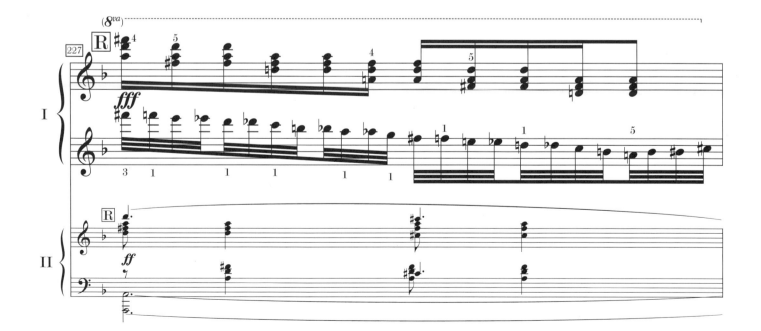

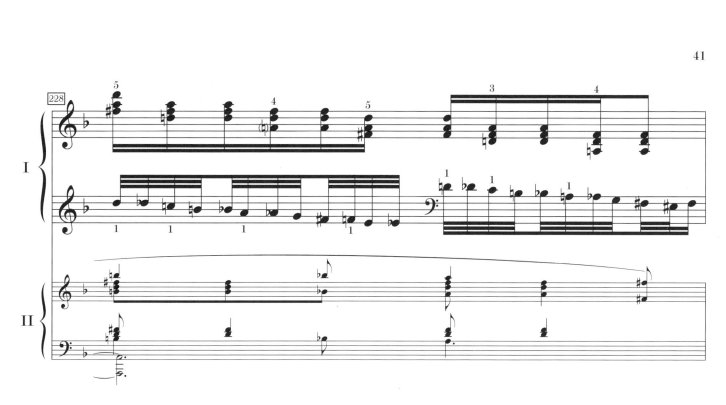

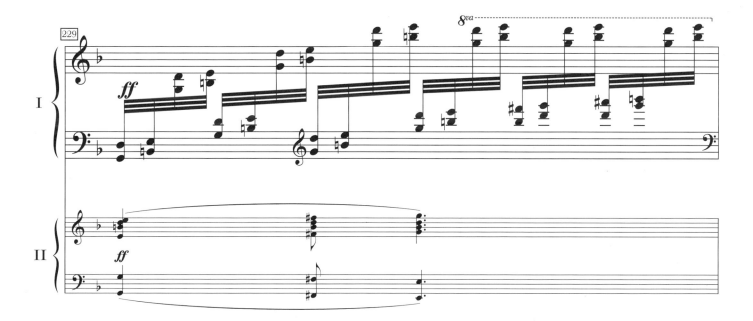

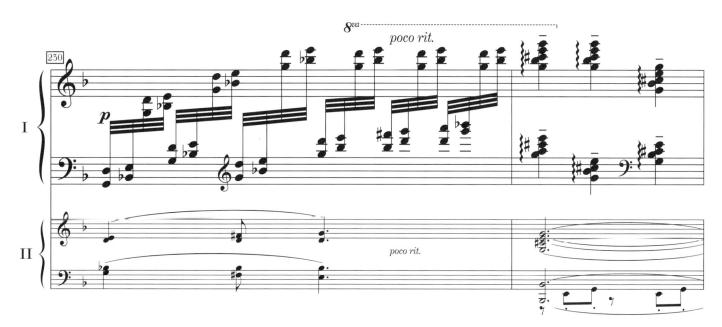

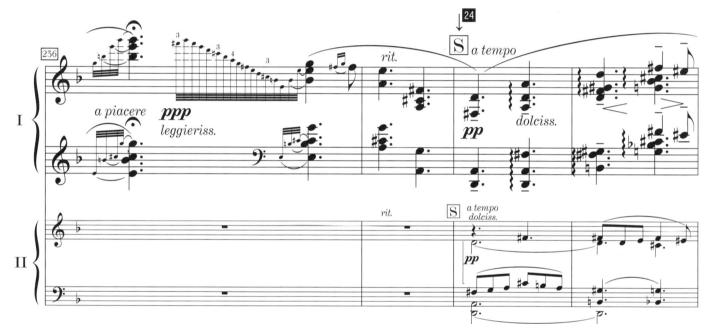

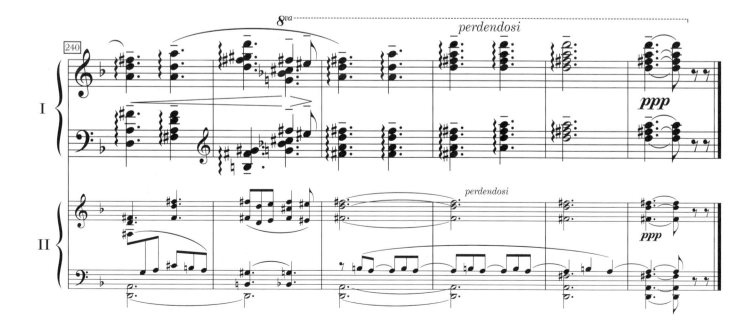

II.

*) The second movement, marked *Presto giocoso*, is often played too slowly for its proper effect. The recommended ♩=160
  is correct, in my opinion, but difficult to maintain. Orchestras seem to want to play it a bit slower and can drag the pianist down.
  Don't let it happen! ♩=152 still works fine, but slower than that and the character suffers.

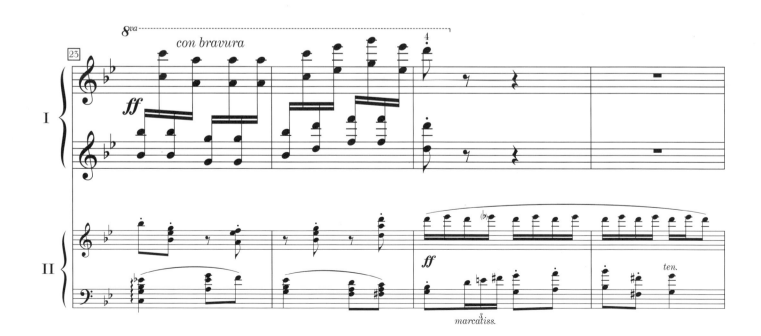

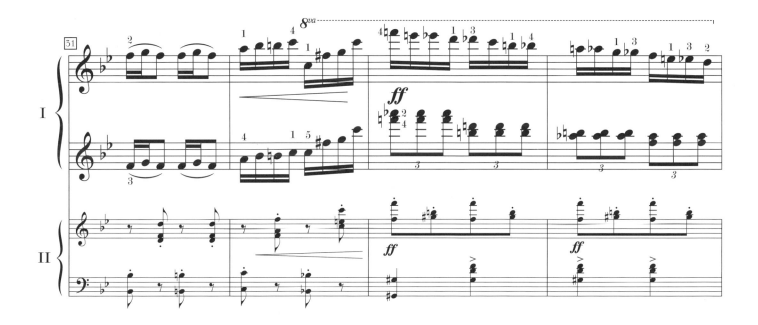

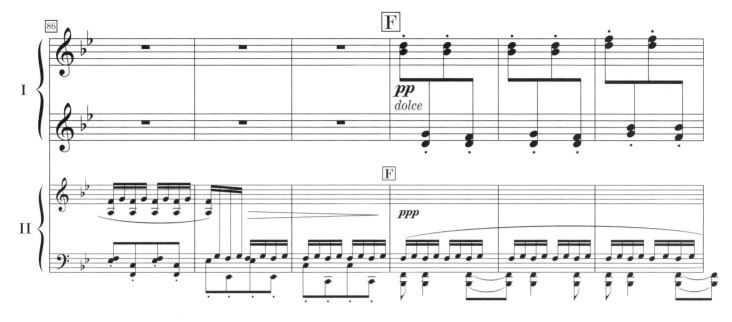

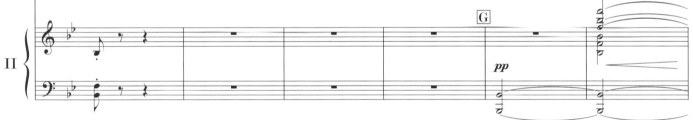

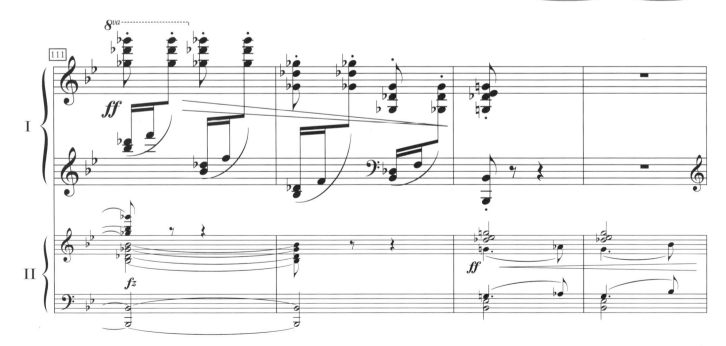

*) The *risoluto* passages starting at letter H should not be markedly slower (144 is too slow in my opinion). Vary your touch between *legato* and *non-legato* in the running passages and don't be afraid to play with the dynamics in order to bring variety and joy to your performance.

52

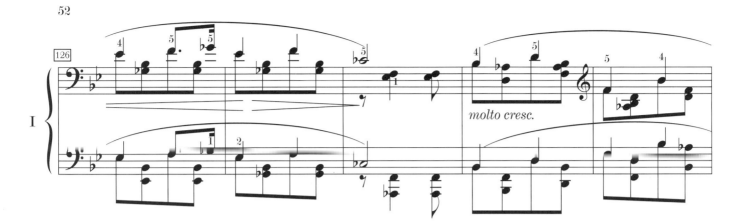

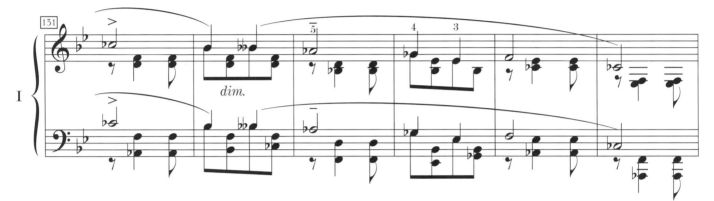

MMO 3090

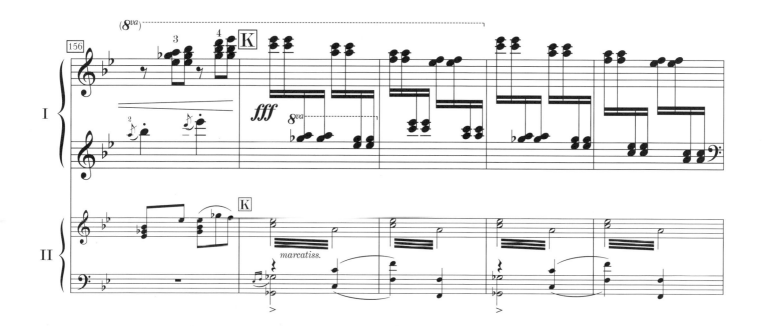

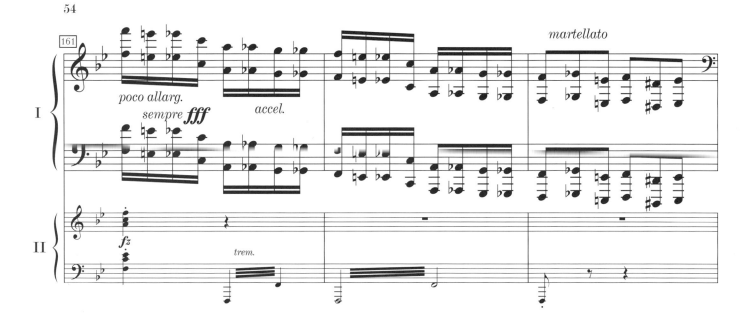

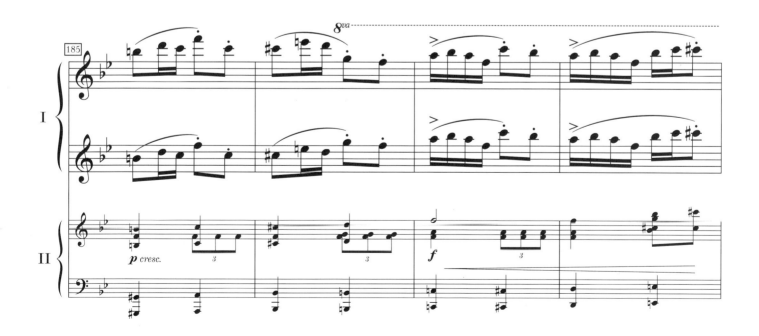

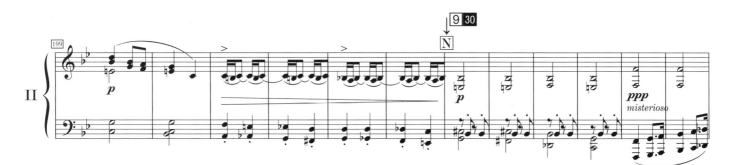

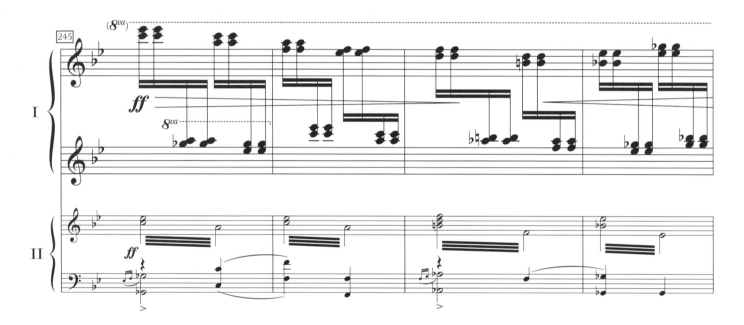

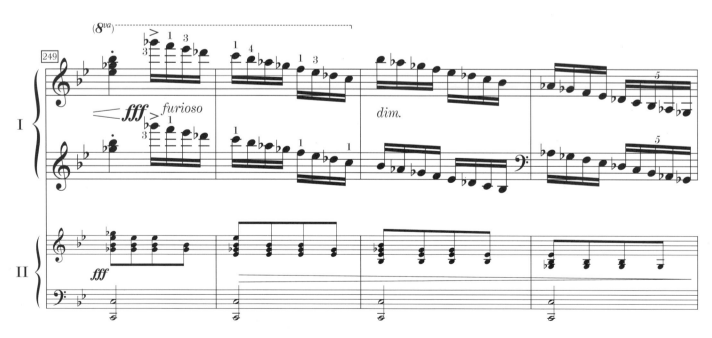

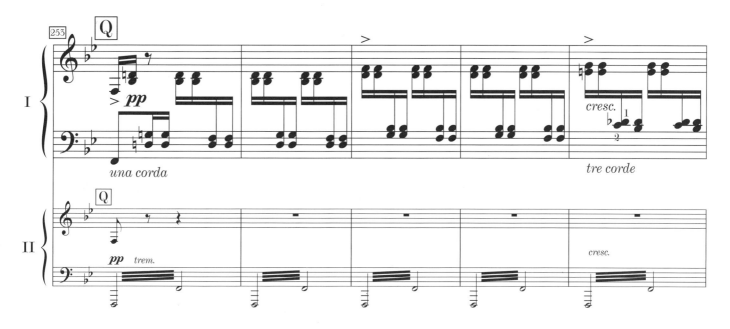

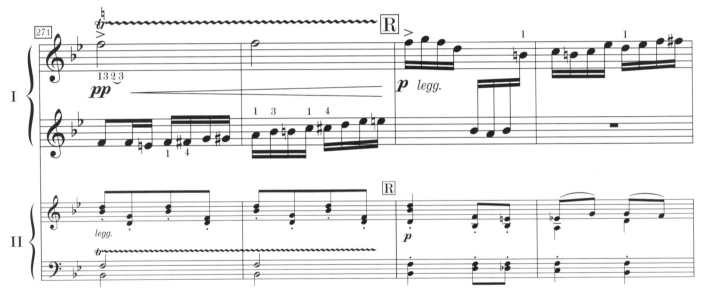

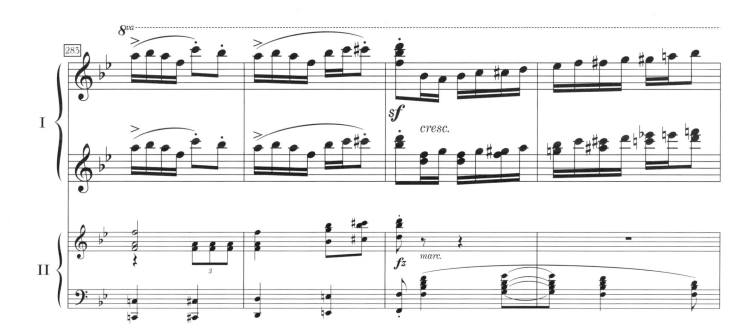

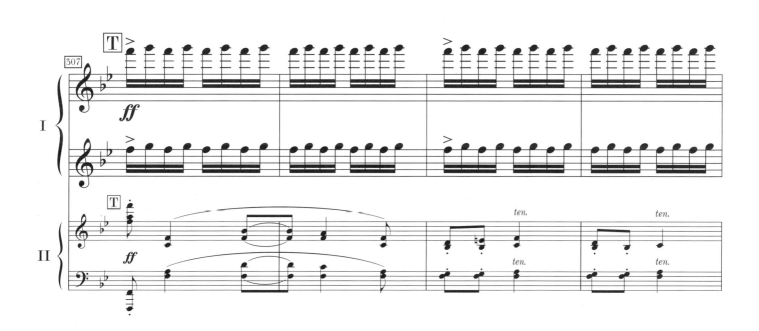

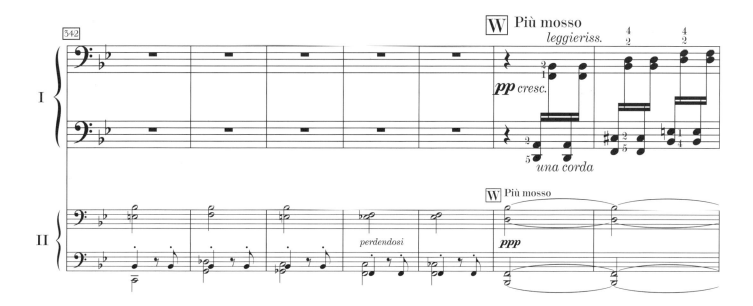

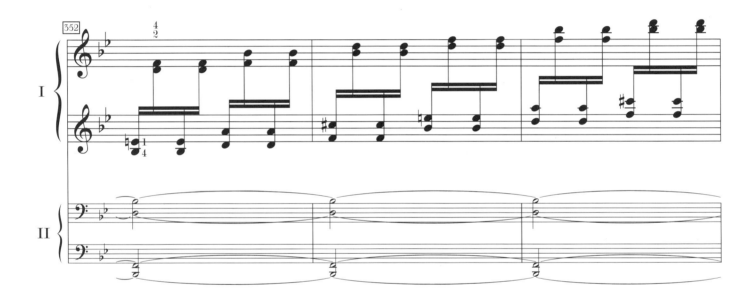

III.

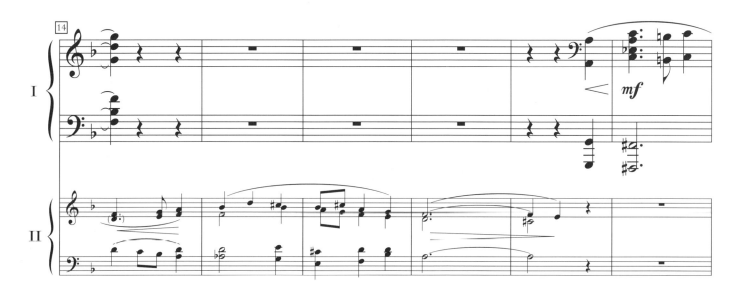

*) The final movement, begins *Largo*, i.e. broadly, and refers back to the opening movement's melodic and dramatic themes.
It should not be too slow.

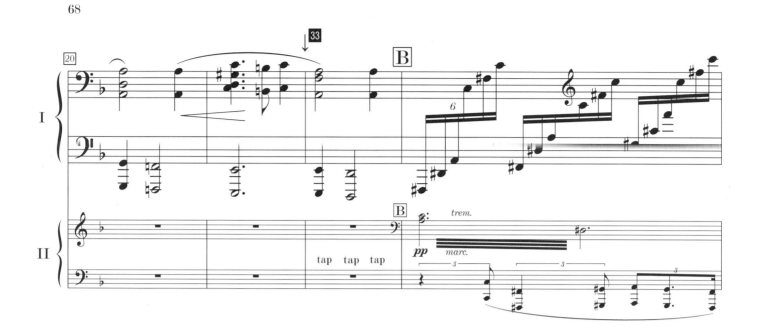

*) I believe that MacDowell's marking of *Forte* at bar 27 indicates that this reference to the opening should not be played quite as powerfully or tragically as in the first movement. We are moving rapidly into a whirlwind of optimism and good cheer!

*) The scales at bar 41 through letter D must be taken in tempo. At a dotted half note=84-88, Edwin Hughes' traditional
   scale fingerings just didn't work for me. I devised my alternate approach, which ultimately proved successful.

**) At bar 51, explore many fingerings if mine don't work and find something that will keep the tempo pretty much without *ritenuto*.
   Good luck!

*) At bar 55, don't hesitate to omit the lower c'♯ in the right-hand octave if you need to. No one will miss it and it may add clarity to the line.

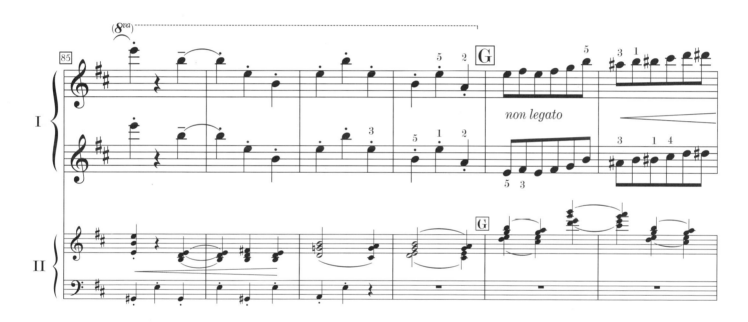

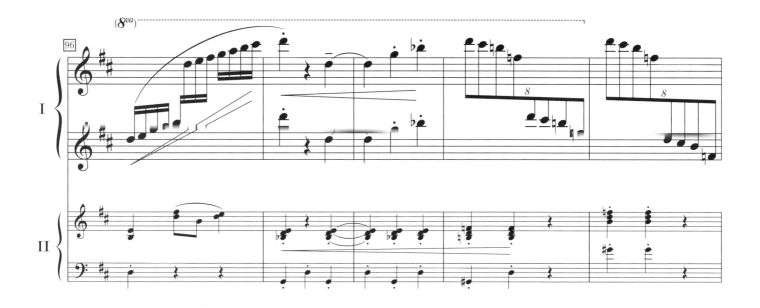

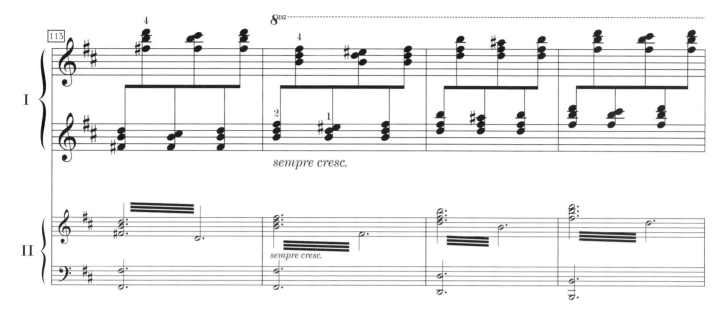

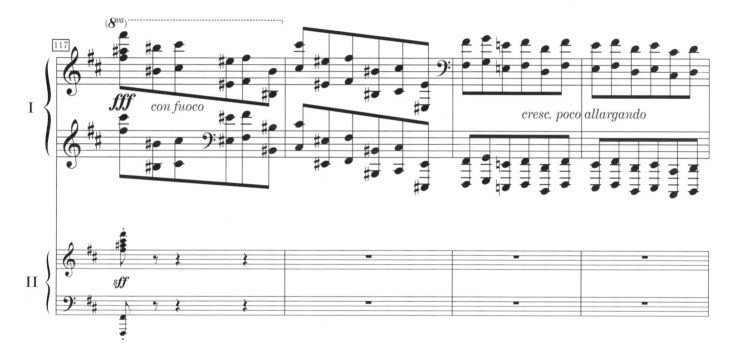

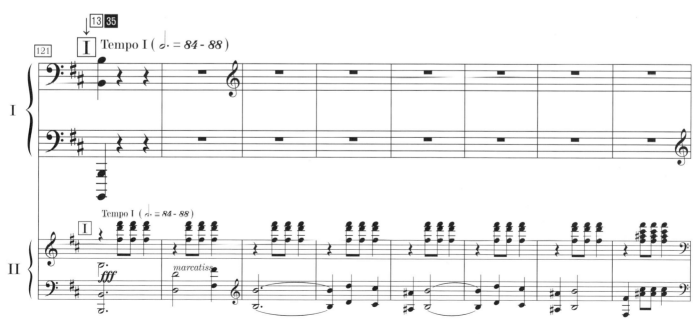

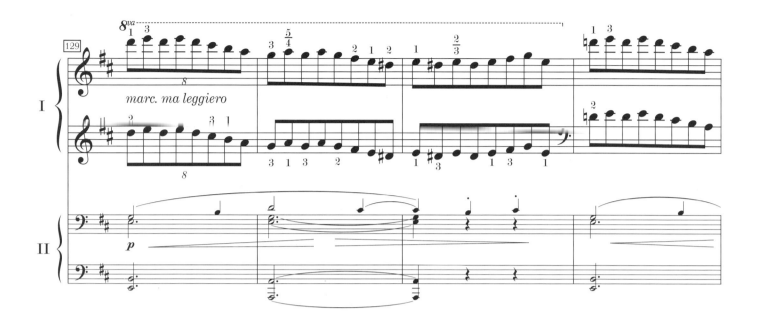

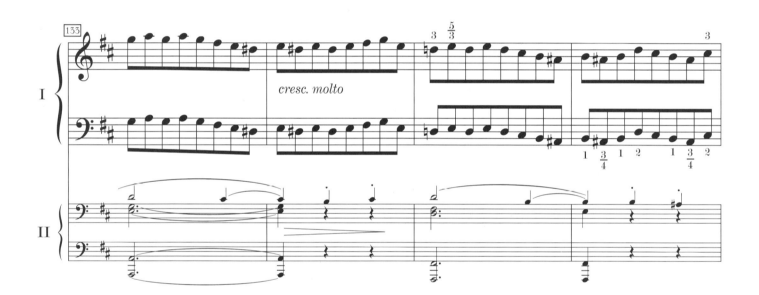

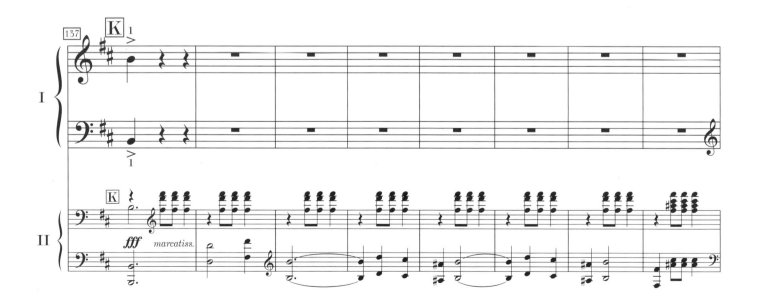

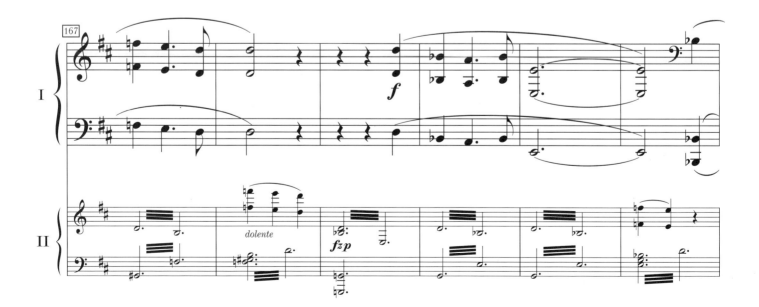

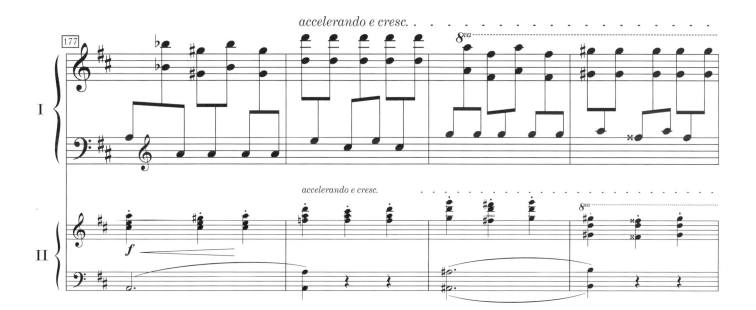

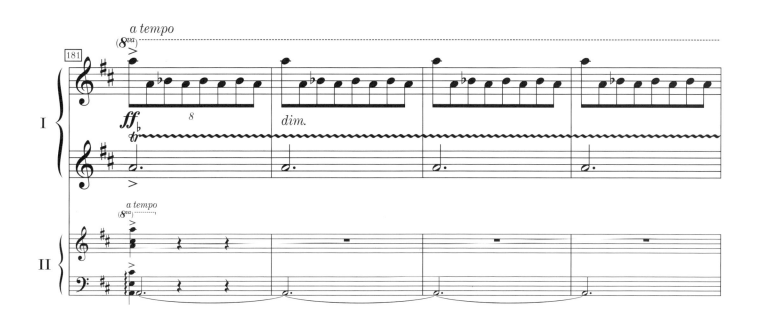

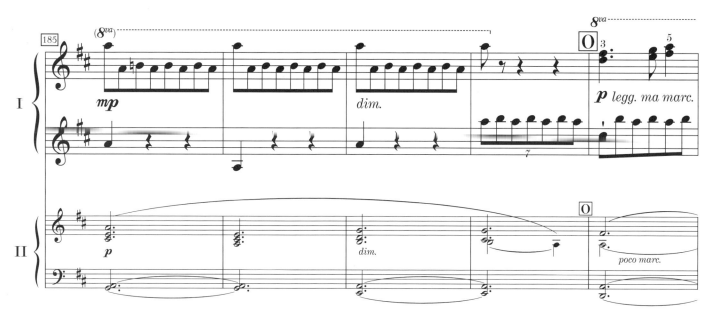

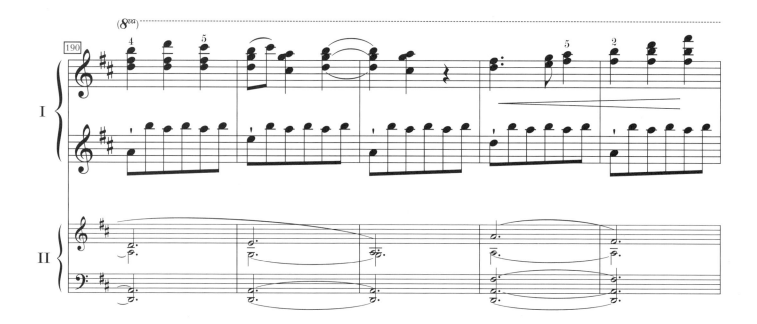

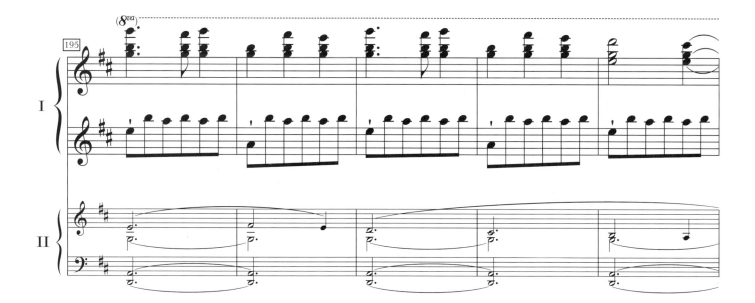

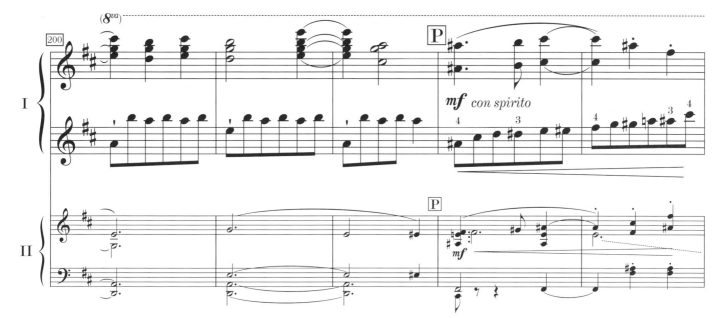

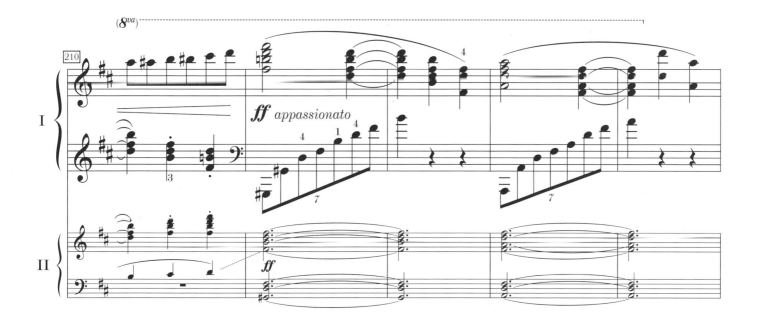

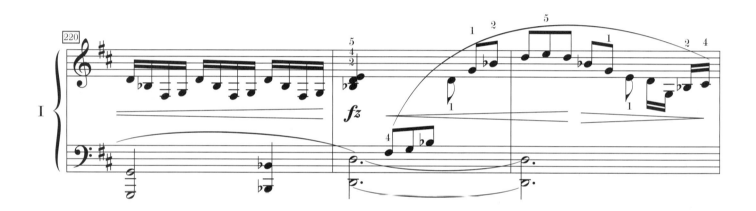

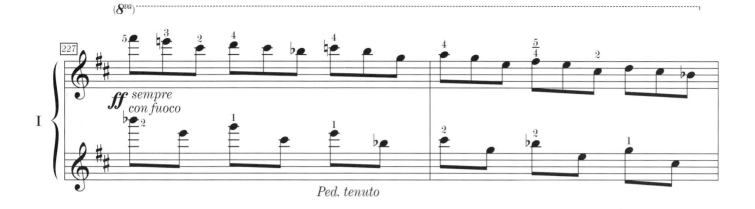

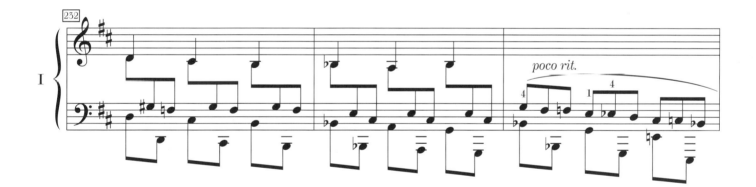

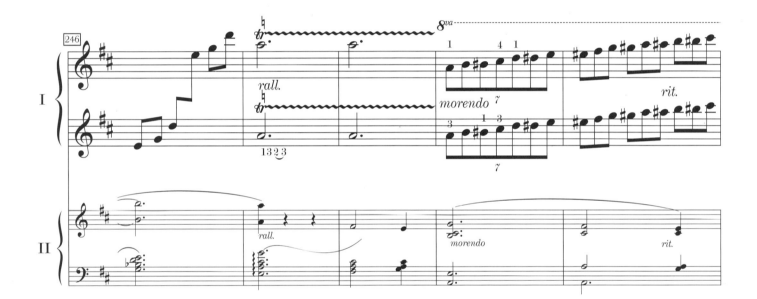

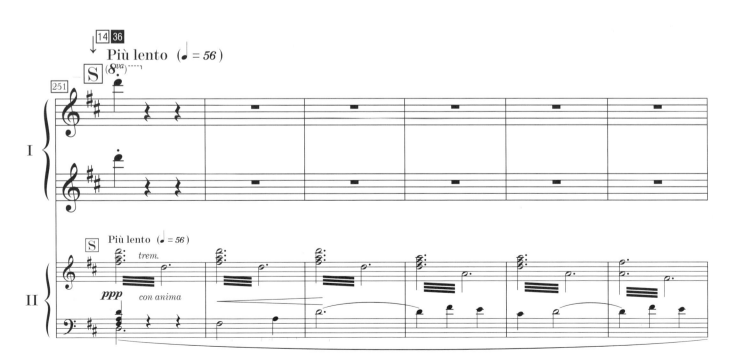

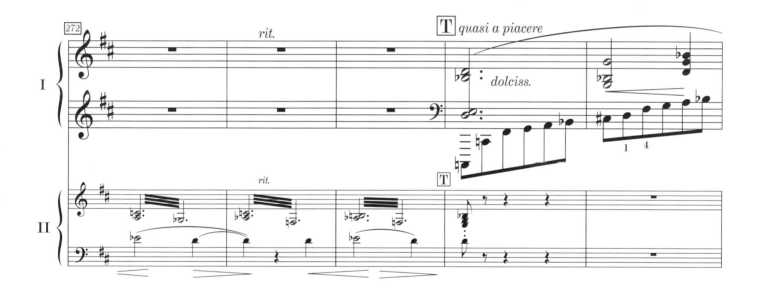

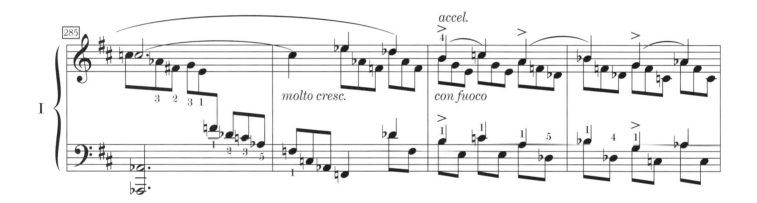

*) Bars 289-290 are tricky for ensemble: First, there is a *hemiola* effect, with two groups of three beats, and at the same time, an *accelerando* to a tempo. It's hard to get it right with the orchestra. Practice from bar 290 on with a metronome until you automatically play the right tempo, then practice the *accelerando* into it so that bar 289 is already at that speed. Good luck!

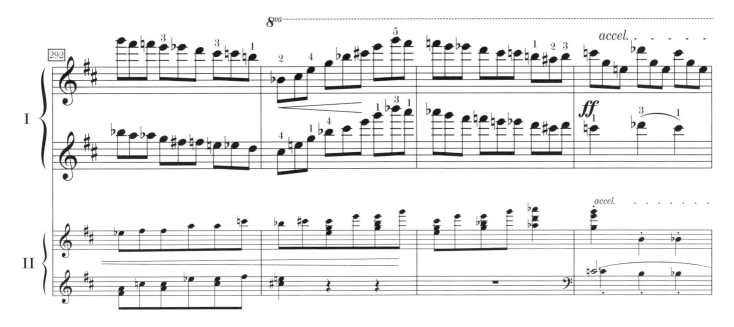

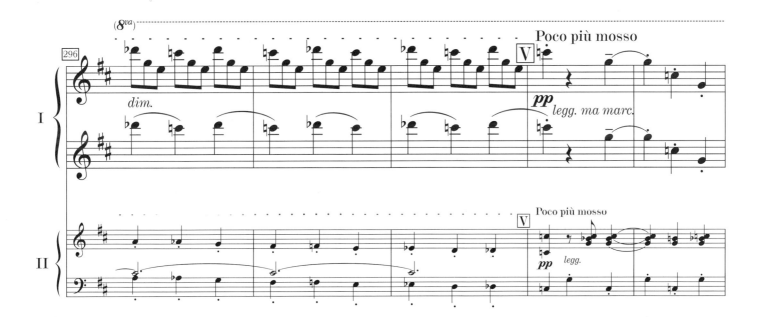

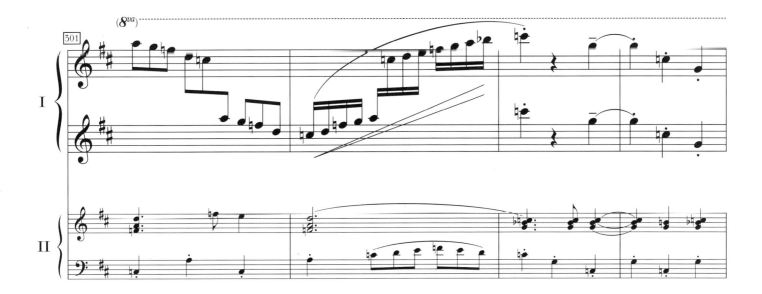

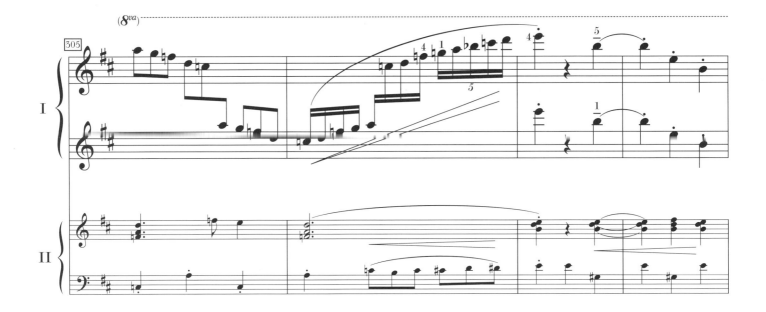

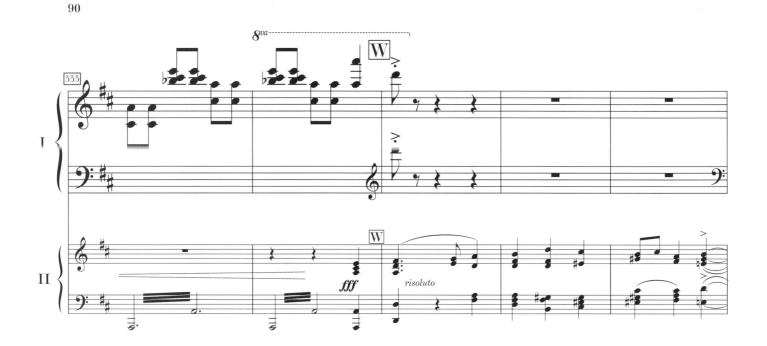

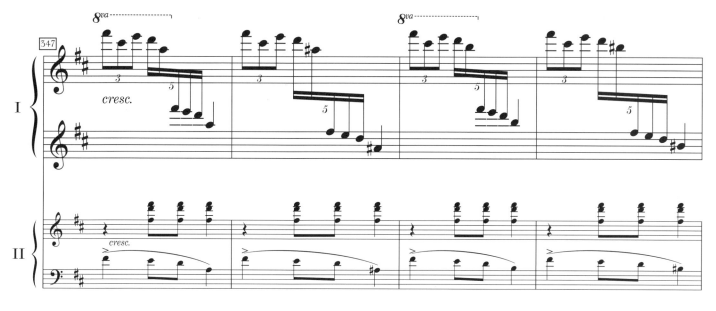

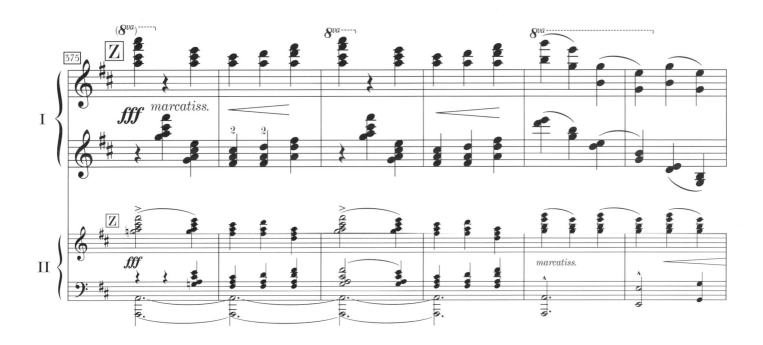

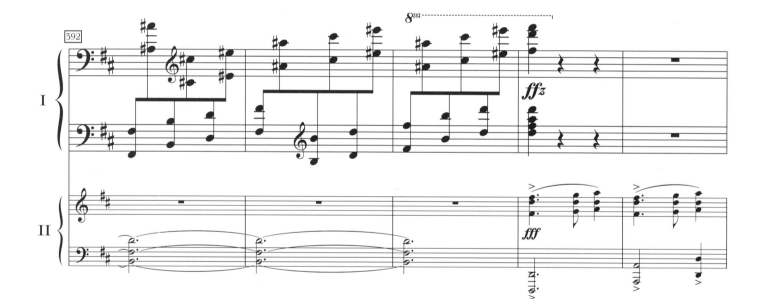

Prestissimo

*) This funny anticipation of the final chord sounds better, in my view, if played as a quarter note. It sounds early enough to be
recognized as support to the orchestral sound and enough that it will (hopefully!) not be taken as an end-of-the-show blunder!

Engraving: Wieslaw Novak

MUSIC MINUS ONE
50 Executive Boulevard
Elmsford, New York 10523-1325
800-669-7464 (U.S.)/914-592-1188 (International)

www.musicminusone.com
e-mail: mmogroup@musicminusone.com

MMO 3090

Printed in Canada